Vocabulary
Workbook

SOCIAL STUDIES

SCOTT FORESMAN

SCOTT FORESMAN

REGIONS

PEARSON

Scott
Foresman

Editorial Offices: Glenview, Illinois • Parsippany, New Jersey • New York, New York
Sales Offices: Parsippany, New Jersey • Duluth, Georgia • Glenview, Illinois
Coppell, Texas • Ontario, California • Mesa, Arizona

www.sfsocialstudies.com

ISBN 0-328-09067-0

Copyright © Pearson Education, Inc.

4 5 6 7 8 9 10 V011 12 11 10 09 08 07 06 05

Count the Syllables

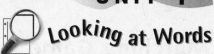
Looking at Words

Write each vocabulary word from the word box in the box below that corresponds to the correct number of syllables. You may use your glossary to help you.

region	mountain	desert	plateau	climate
landform	plain	canyon	boundary	weather
precipitation	temperature	equator	humidity	

1 Syllable

_____

3 Syllables

_____

_____

2 Syllables

_____

_____

_____

_____

_____

_____

4 Syllables

_____

_____

5 Syllables

_____

Notes for Home: Your child counted the number of syllables in some of the vocabulary words in this unit.
Home Activity: Have your child read the rest of the vocabulary words from the unit to you and count the syllables in each one.

Matching Game

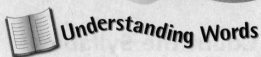
Understanding Words

Play this game with a partner. Each player needs a set of vocabulary cards on which is written his or her name.

Player 1: Stack all your vocabulary cards in a pile, word side up.

Player 2: Place all your vocabulary cards in a line, in any order, with the definition side up.

Player 1: Take the top card from the stack of cards with the word side up. Find the definition you feel matches the word. If the word and definition match, take the pair. If not, put the word card at the bottom of the stack and the definition card back in the line.

Player 2: Repeat the same steps as Player 1.

Keep playing by taking turns until there are no more cards to match. The player who has the most pairs at the end of the game is the winner.

Repeat the game until each player can match all the words and definitions. Then each player is a winner!

Notes for Home: Your child matched vocabulary cards with definitions.
Home Activity: With your child, go over these words from this unit: *region, landform, boundary, weather, climate, natural resource, raw material, industry, capital resource, renewable resource, recycle, immigrant, culture, democracy, citizen, Constitution, federal, taxes, rural, urban, producer, consumer, supply, demand, interdependent, globalization,* and *communication.* Have your child give you his or her own explanations of the words and then tell how they relate to the subjects of the unit.

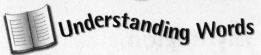

UNIT 1

One Nation, Indivisible

Understanding Words

Choose the vocabulary word or term from the box that completes each sentence. Write the word on the line in the sentence. Use your glossary if you need help.

Capitol	**democracy**	**Supreme Court**	**executive branch**
citizen	**White House**	**amendment**	**legislative branch**
passport	**Bill of Rights**	**Constitution**	**judicial branch**

1. I'm glad I live in a _____, where I can vote in a fair election.

2. The head of the _____ is the President.

3. Trials are heard by the _____ of government.

4. He has rights because he is a _____ of the United States.

5. Freedom of the press was guaranteed by an _____ to the Constitution.

6. The _____ are the first ten amendments to the Constitution.

7. The _____ is the supreme law of the United States.

8. You can visit the _____ to see Congress in action.

9. The _____ is the home of the President.

10. The nine judges on the _____ are appointed for life.

11. Tax laws are made by the _____ of government.

12. She showed her _____ to the agent so she could board the plane to Europe.

Notes for Home: Your child learned vocabulary words about our government and the rights and responsibilities of citizens.
Home Activity: Ask your child to explain each word to you by using a real-world example.

© Scott Foresman 4

My Region

Expository Writing

Each region of the United States is interesting and unique. What makes your region special? Think about the special features that make your region a great place to live. Write a paragraph to describe your region and the things that make it unique. Use as many words from the word box as you can. You may use an additional sheet of paper.

region	landform	mountain	plain	desert
canyon	plateau	weather	climate	precipitation
temperature	humidity	elevation	harvest	manufacturing
industry	agriculture	service		
immigrant	culture	natural resource		

_____

_____

_____

_____

_____

_____

_____

_____

_____

_____

Notes for Home: Your child wrote a paragraph to describe the unique features of your region.
Home Activity: Discuss with your child the things visitors to your region like to see and do. Look at local travel agencies or visitor's bureaus to find information on local attractions.

region

landform

mountain

plain

desert

canyon

plateau

a natural feature of the earth's surface

a large area in which places share similar characteristics

an area of flat land that often is covered with grass or trees

a very high landform, often with steep sides

a deep valley with steep rocky walls

an area that receives less than ten inches of rain in one year

a large, flat, raised area of land

boundary

weather

climate

precipitation

temperature

humidity

equator

the condition of the air at a certain time and place

a line or natural feature that separates one area or state from another

the amount of moisture that falls as rain or snow

the weather patterns in one place over a long period of time

the amount of moisture in the air

a measurement telling how hot or cold something is

the imaginary line that circles the center of Earth from east to west

elevation

tropical climate

polar climate

subarctic climate

temperate climate

natural resource

raw material

an area that is usually very warm all year	how high a place is above sea level
an area with short, warm summers and ground covered in snow for most of the rest of the year	areas around the North and South Poles with the coldest temperatures
something in the environment that can be used	moderate area between tropical and subarctic climates
	something that is changed so that people can use it

process

harvest

industry

manufacturing

product

capital resource

agriculture

cut for use as a crop

to change something so that people can use it

making things to use or sell

a business that makes a product or provides a service

something people make in order to produce other products

something that people make or grow

the raising of crops or animals

✂

conserve

renewable resource

recycle

nonrenewable resource

human resource

service

immigrant

a natural resource that can
be replaced

to use resources carefully

a resource that cannot be replaced

to use something more than once

job that someone does for others

a person who makes products or
provides services

a person who comes to live in a
new land

culture

government

republic

represent

democracy

citizen

Constitution

the laws that are followed and the people that run a country

a way of life followed by a group of people

the act of leaders making decisions for those who elected them

a type of government in which people elect leaders to represent them

an official member of a country

a system of government in which every citizen has a right to take part

the written plan for governing the United States of America

✂

federal	**legislative branch**
Capitol	**executive branch**
White House	**judicial branch**
Supreme Court	

the part of government that
makes laws

a system of government in which
the national and state governments
share power

the part of government that
enforces the laws

the building where the Congress
of the United States meets

the part of government made
up of courts and judges, that
interprets laws

the place where the President of
the United States lives and works

the highest court of the
United States

amendment

Bill of Rights

passport

taxes

jury

technology

the list of rights the United States government guarantees to its citizens

a change to the Constitution of the United States

money the government collects to pay for its services

a paper or booklet that gives a person permission to travel to other countries

the development and use of scientific knowledge to solve practical problems

a panel of ordinary citizens who make decisions in a court of law

rural	**urban**
need	**want**
barter	**producer**

© Scott Foresman 4

in the city

in small towns or farms

something that a person would like to have but can live without

something that a person must have in order to live

a person who makes goods or products to sell

trading one kind of good or service for another

consumer

economy

free enterprise system

profit

supply

demand

the way in which the resources of a country, state, region, or community are managed

a person who buys goods and services

the money left over after costs are paid

a system in which businesses have the right to produce any good or provide any service that they want

the amount of an item that consumers are willing to buy at different prices

the amount of an item someone has to sell

opportunity cost

transportation

interdependent

globalization

communication

the moving of goods, people, or animals from one place to another

what is given up when one thing is chosen over another

the process by which a business makes something or provides a service in different places around the world

when regions rely on one another for goods, services, or resources

the way that people send and receive information

Name _____

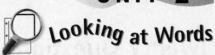

Predicting Meaning

A compound word is a word that is made up of two or more words. If you know the meaning of each word in the compound, it can help you predict its meaning. *Bathtub* is a compound made up of the words *bath* and *tub*.

bath +	*tub* =	*bathtub*
"a washing of the body with water"	"a large, wide, deep container"	"a large, wide, deep container that is used for washing the body"

Using what you know about the smaller words, predict the meaning of each vocabulary word by writing a definition in your own words. Check the vocabulary cards to see how well you did in your prediction.

lighthouse   vineyard   inlet   watermen

1. light + house = lighthouse
The meaning of **lighthouse** could be _____

_____.

2. vine + yard = vineyard
The meaning of **vineyard** could be _____

_____.

3. in + let = inlet
The meaning of **inlet** could be _____

_____.

4. water + men = watermen
The meaning of **watermen** could be _____

_____.

 Notes for Home: Your child used knowledge of familiar words to predict the meanings of compound words.
Home Activity: Have your child use a dictionary to predict the meanings of other compound words related to school and home, such as *homework, blackboard, classroom, schoolteacher, toothpaste, bedspread, bookcase,* and *floorboard.*

Name _____

Twenty Questions

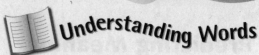

Understanding Words

Work with a partner. Use one set of vocabulary cards. Place all of the cards in a container. Player 1 draws a card and holds it so Player 2 cannot see it. Player 2 can ask twenty "yes" or "no" questions to try to figure out what vocabulary word Player 1 is holding. Players switch roles each time.

As you play, be sure to tally the number of questions you ask. When you have guessed the word, or asked all twenty questions, write down the word in the blank and the number of questions it took to guess it. If you were unable to guess the word, your score for that word is 25.

When each player has guessed five words, add up the total number of questions you asked. The player who asked the **least** number of questions is the winner.

Player 1

Word	Questions
1.	
2.	
3.	
4.	
5.	
Total	

Player 2

Word	Questions
1.	
2.	
3.	
4.	
5.	
Total	

Notes for Home: Today your child reviewed the meanings of the vocabulary words by playing a guessing game with a partner.
Home Activity: Ask your child to use this unit's vocabulary words to describe life among the Narragansett Indians at the time the first Europeans arrived.

Vocabulary Workbook

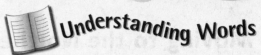

UNIT 2

Understanding Words

Break Down the Words

The vocabulary words below all begin with a prefix. When a prefix is added to the beginning of a word, a base, or phrase, the prefix changes its meaning. Let's look at the word *import*.

prefix: *im-*   meaning: "in," "within," "into," "on," or "toward"

base: *port*   meaning: from the Latin word *portare* (pronounced pohr-TAR-ee), which means "to carry"

Put the meanings of *im-* and *port* together and you have the meaning of **import,** which is "to carry in." In noun form, an **import** is an item "carried in" from another country to be offered for sale.

import	**hydroelectricity**	**cooperation**
export	**hydropower**	

1. Each pair of definitions below defines a prefix and the word or base whose meaning it changes. Write the vocabulary word from the box above that matches each pair of definitions.

   water + energy _____

   together + performance of work _____

   water + form of power found in nature _____

   out of + to carry _____

2. Based on your answers above, give definitions for the prefixes below.

   hydro- _____

   ex- _____

   co- _____

Notes for Home: Your child broke down words into their parts by learning the definitions of some prefixes.
Home Activity: Read pages from a book, magazine, or newspaper with your child. As you read them, have your child identify words that begin with the prefixes *im-, in-, ex-, hydro-,* and *co-*.

Moving to the Northeast

Narrative Writing

The Northeast is a place of many natural wonders and resources. Think about the things you would see and feel if you visited or lived in this region. Write a letter to a friend to describe the Northeast. Use at least four words from the word box. You may use an additional sheet of paper.

gorge	hydropower	peninsula	vineyard	mineral
diverse	hydroelectricity	watermen	bog	inlet
lighthouse	bay	crab pot	sap	quarry

_____

_____

_____

_____

_____

_____

_____

_____

_____

_____

_____

_____

_____

_____

Notes for Home: Your child used vocabulary words to describe things they might see while in the Northeast.
Home Activity: Have your child select one of the vocabulary words he or she used in writing. Together, look up information about the physical feature or resource.

glacier

gorge

hydropower

hydroelectricity

lighthouse

peninsula

vineyard

bog

a deep narrow valley

huge sheets of ice that cover land

electricity produced by
flowing water

power produced by capturing the
energy of flowing water

a piece of land almost surrounded
by water

a tall tower with a very strong light
used to guide ships

an area of soft, wet, spongy ground

a place where grapevines
are planted

sap

mineral

quarry

bay

inlet

watermen

crab pot

cooperation

metal or other resource dug from the ground

a liquid carrying water and food that circulates through a plant

part of a sea or lake that cuts into a coastline

a place where stone is dug, cut, or blasted out of the ground

men or women who gather different kinds of seafood and fish in different seasons

a narrow opening in a coastline

to work together to get things done

a large wire cage with several sections that crabs swim into but from which they cannot escape

✂

wigwam

sachem

reservation

powwow

confederacy

colony

revolution

a ruler over a portion of
Narragansett territory

a Narragansett hut made of
wooden poles covered in bark

a Native American festival

an area of land set aside
by the United States for
Native Americans

a settlement of people who
come from one country to live
in another land

a union of groups, countries, or
states that agree to work together
for a common goal

a fight to overthrow a government

✂

abolitionist	**slave**
convention	**commerce**
import	**export**
diverse	

a person who is owned as property by another person and is forced to work

a reformer who believed that slavery should be erased from the law

the buying and selling of goods, especially in large amounts between different places

a meeting place held for a certain purpose

an item sent from one country to be sold in another

an item brought from abroad to be offered for sale

varied

UNIT 3

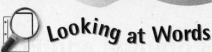

Break It Up

You can learn to read and spell new words, short or long, when you break them into syllables. Remember, a syllable is a part of a word in which we hear a vowel sound. Here are some examples of how words can be broken into syllables:

- Break between double consonants. Example: *bar – ri – er.*
- Sometimes break between two different consonants. Example: *pen – cil.*
- Sometimes a vowel stands alone. Example: *math – e – mat – ics.*

Write each vocabulary word below in syllables. Use a dictionary to check your answers.

1. **backwoodsman** _____

2. **endangered species** _____

3. **hurricane** _____

4. **public transportation system** _____

5. **civil rights** _____

6. **fossil fuel** _____

7. **pioneer** _____

8. **consensus** _____

9. **plantation** _____

10. **segregate** _____

11. **secede** _____

12. **extinct** _____

13. **boycott** _____

Notes for Home: Your child learned to read words by breaking them into syllables.
Home Activity: With your child, look at newspapers or magazines and break up the long words into syllables.

Common and Proper Nouns

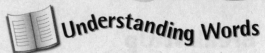

Understanding Words

Common nouns give general names for people, places, or things. Proper nouns name specific people, places, or things. Proper nouns are easy to identify because they begin with a capital letter. Read the vocabulary words in the box. Write each common noun next to its proper example. Write each proper noun next to its common example.

pioneer	Trail of Tears	Civil War	Reconstruction
gold rush	Confederacy	Union	

Common	**Proper**
1. war	_____
2. _____	Daniel Boone
3. northern states	_____
4. forced journey	_____
5. rebuilding period	_____
6. _____	California Gold Rush
7. southern states	_____

Write a proper noun from the unit to match the common nouns.

8. state	_____
9. country	_____
10. leader	_____

Notes for Home: Your child learned to identify common and proper nouns in the vocabulary from this unit.
Home Activity: Invite your child to explain how he or she determined which nouns were proper or common in this exercise. Together, come up with other common and proper noun pairs.

Name _____

Using Vocabulary

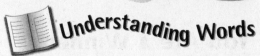

Understanding Words

Choose the vocabulary word that belongs in each sentence and write it on the blank. Then add a sentence of your own that tells something more about, or gives an example of, the vocabulary word.

| barrier islands | key | fall line | fossil fuel |
| hurricane season | pulp | wetlands | |

1. Violent storms are expected during _____.

_____

2. Off the coast of North Carolina are _____, landforms

formed over thousands of years from deposited material in the ocean.

_____

3. The _____ boundary is known for its tumbling waters.

_____

4. Trees are turned into _____ to make paper.

_____

5. A _____ is an energy source formed in the earth.

_____

6. Marshes, swamps, and bogs are examples of _____.

_____

7. A low piece of land surrounded by water is a _____.

_____

Notes for Home: Today your child used some of this unit's vocabulary words in original sentences.
Home Activity: Together with your child, write one more sentence that tells something about, or gives an example of, each of the vocabulary words used in this activity.

You Are a Winner!

Expository Writing

You have learned a great deal about the variety and beauty of the Southeast.
Suppose you won a trip to visit any part of the Southeast you wanted. Which area
would it be? Write a paragraph to describe the features of this area of the Southeast
that make it the part you most want to see and explore. Use as many vocabulary
words as you can. You may use an additional sheet of paper.

barrier islands	wetlands	fall line	key
hurricane season	plantation	endangered species	
hurricane	extinct	public transportation system	

_____

_____

_____

_____

_____

_____

_____

_____

_____

_____

_____

_____

 Notes for Home: Today your child wrote about a particular part of the Southeast that he or
she would like to visit.
Home Activity: Using the Internet or local travel services, help your child find information on
the location he or she chose. Read together about what types of things visitors like to do there.

barrier islands

wetlands

fall line

key

hurricane

hurricane season

land that is covered with water at times

a narrow island between the ocean and the mainland

a low island

a line of waterfalls that marks the boundary between the Piedmont and the coastal plains

the time of the year when hurricanes mainly occur

a violent storm with high winds and heavy rain that forms over an ocean

✂

endangered species	extinct
pulp	**fossil fuel**
consensus	**Trail of Tears**

no longer existing

a kind of animal or plant that is in danger of becoming extinct

a fuel formed in the earth from the remains of plants and animals

a combination of wood chips, water, and chemicals used to make paper

the forced journey of the Cherokees to land set aside for them by the United States in what is now Oklahoma

a method of decision-making in which all come to agreement

✂

pioneer	backwoodsman
plantation	Civil War
Union	Confederacy

Name _____

a person who lives in forests or wild areas far away from towns

a person who settles in a part of a country and prepares it for others

the United States Civil War, fought between Northern and Southern states from 1861 to 1865

a large farm that produces crops to sell

the name for the Southern states in the United States Civil War

the name for the Northern states during the American Civil War

Vocabulary Workbook

secede

Reconstruction

civil rights

segregate

gold rush

public transportation system

the period of time after the United
States Civil War when the South
was rebuilt

to pull out of or separate from

to separate people according to
their race

the rights of a citizen, including
the right to vote and protection
under the law

the trains and buses that carry
people through a city

a sudden movement of people to
an area where gold has been found

Good Guides

Words in a dictionary are listed in alphabetical order. Guide words at the top of each page tell you the first and last words on the page. Using guide words can help you find the word you are looking for more quickly. Alphabetize your vocabulary cards. Then write each vocabulary word under its correct guide words. For example, *muffin* would be under "mill–sour" because *mu* is between *mi* and *s* in alphabetical order.

1. back–cart

_____

_____

_____

2. count–dug

_____

_____

3. dull–invite

_____

_____

_____

_____

4. iron–might

_____

_____

5. mill–sour

_____

_____

_____

6. stack–wave

_____

_____

_____

_____

> **Notes for Home:** Your child practiced using guide words.
> **Home Activity:** Help your child use guide words to find other vocabulary words from this unit in a dictionary.

The Suffixes -ion and -ation

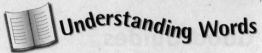 Understanding Words

When you add the suffix *-ion* or *-ation* to a verb, the verb becomes a noun.

Root Word (Verb)	Add Suffix	Noun
add	+ -ion →	addition

We <u>add</u> the numbers.   Be sure to check your <u>addition</u>.

| combine | + -ation → | combination |

We will <u>combine</u> our money   Chocolate syrup and milk
to buy the new game.   is a tasty <u>combination</u>.

For numbers 1–4, find the root word that forms the noun in the right-hand column. The first three words are vocabulary words from this unit. For numbers 5–8, find the noun that is created when *-ion* or *-ation* is added to the root word. You may use a dictionary to help you.

Root Word (Verb)	Add *-ion* or *-ation* (Noun)
1. _____	**erosion**
2. _____	**rotation**
3. _____	**irrigation**
4. _____	starvation
5. act	_____
6. donate	_____
7. invite	_____
8. locate	_____

 Notes for Home: Today your child created nouns from verbs and found root words of nouns by adding and removing the suffixes *-ion* and *-ation*.
Home Activity: Have your child write other verbs that can be changed into nouns by adding the suffixes *-ion* and *-ation*.

© Scott Foresman 4

Traveling Words

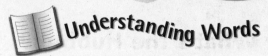
Understanding Words

Some of the vocabulary words in the word box are related to transportation on land. Others are related to transportation on water. Sort the words by writing each one in the correct category.

transcontinental railroad	steamboat	barge	waterway
Interstate highway system	canal	lock	

Travel by Land	Travel by Water
_____	_____
_____	_____
_____	_____
_____	_____
_____	_____
_____	_____

Notes for Home: Today your child sorted vocabulary words about the development of transportation in the Midwest to reinforce the meaning of the words.
Home Activity: Have your child increase his or her knowledge of transportation words by talking about different means of transportation that family members may have used, such as a bus, plane, subway, or ferry.

Name _____

What's the Hubbub?

Expository Writing

The ability to transport goods became easier in the United States in the 1800s. Two Midwestern cities—Chicago and St. Louis—benefited from their central location and developments in transportation. In the 1800s, suppose you needed to ship goods from New York City to a destination in the Midwest. How would you ship your goods? Write to describe how your goods would travel and what cities they would travel through to reach their destination. Use at least four of the vocabulary words. You may use an additional sheet of paper.

steamboat	barge	lock
transcontinental railroad	hub	canal

_____

_____

_____

_____

_____

_____

_____

_____

_____

_____

_____

_____

_____

 Notes for Home: Today your child used vocabulary words to describe how goods might travel in the 1800s to the Midwest.
Home Activity: Look at a highway map of your state or any state. Using the map, help your child locate major hubs. Discuss why these locations have turned into hubs.

　　　　　　　　　　　　　　　　　　　　Vocabulary Workbook

© Scott Foresman 4

waterway

canal

lock

barge

badlands

erosion

prairie

a waterway that has been dug across land for ships to travel through

a system of rivers, lakes, and canals, through which ships travel

a flat-bottomed boat that carries goods through lakes and rivers

a gated part of a canal or river used to raise and lower water levels

the process by which wind and water wear away rock

a region of dry hills and sharp cliffs

an area where grass grows well, but trees are rare

crop rotation

irrigation

fur trade

mission

trading post

sod

drought

the process of bringing water
to crops

the planting of different crops in
different years

a settlement set up by a religious
group to teach religion and help
area people

the trading of goods for
animal skins

the grass, roots, and dirt that form
the ground's top layer

a kind of store in which goods
are traded

a long period with little or no rain

Dust Bowl

mound

steamboat

hub

transcontinental
railroad

Interstate highway
system

© Scott Foresman 4

a pile of earth or stone constructed by early Native Americans for a variety of purposes

an area of the Midwest and Southwest that was struck by years of drought in the 1930s

a center of activity

a boat powered by a steam engine

a system of interconnected highways in the United States

a rail line that crosses an entire country

Singular and Plural Nouns

 Looking at Words

To change a singular noun to a plural, you usually add *-s* or *-es,* depending on the ending sound of the noun. You can use a dictionary to check which ending is correct.

singular:	textbook	**plural:**	textbooks
singular:	lunch	**plural:**	lunches

Some words have special rules. If a word ends in *-y,* drop *-y* and add *-ies.*

singular:	pony	**plural:**	ponies

A Spanish word that ends with *-o* is made plural by adding *-s.*

singular:	amigo (friend)	**plural:**	amigos (friends)

The vocabulary words in the box are singular nouns. Write each vocabulary word in the "Singular" column next to the rule for making that word plural. Then write the plural form of the noun in the "Plural" column.

pueblo	savanna	gusher	refinery	hogan
missionary	vaquero	homestead	aqueduct	

Rule	Singular	Plural
1. Add *-s* or *-es*	_____	_____
	_____	_____
	_____	_____
	_____	_____
	_____	_____
	_____	_____
2. Drop *-y* and add *-ies*	_____	_____
	_____	_____
3. Spanish ending in *-o,* add *-s*	_____	_____
	_____	_____

Notes for Home: Today your child learned to write the singular and plural forms for several of this unit's vocabulary words.
Home Activity: Have your child make a list of the names of objects that they find in their rooms. Have your child write the nouns in groups according to how each singular noun is made into a plural noun by adding *-s, -es,* or *-ies.* Finally, have your child write the plural form of each singular noun.

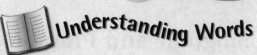

People, Places, and Things

Understanding Words

All the vocabulary words below are nouns. Nouns name people, places, or things.
Use your vocabulary cards to group the words into people, places, and things. Then
write each word in its correct category.

adobe	gusher	viceroy	tallow
pueblo	refinery	missionary	homestead
savanna	hogan	vaquero	aqueduct

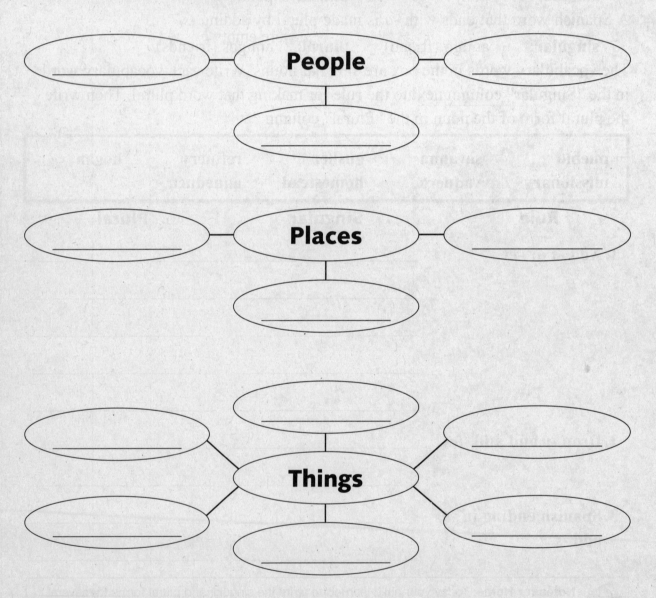

People

Places

Things

Notes for Home: Your child grouped the nouns in the word box into the categories "People,"
"Places," and "Things."
Home Activity: Work with your child to categorize nouns from newspaper or magazine articles
as people, places, or things.

Using Context Clues

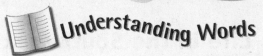
Understanding Words

Read the vocabulary words in the word box. Then read the story. For each blank in the story, write the correct vocabulary word on the line. Use the context clues in the story to identify the correct words.

arid	**missionary**	**adobe**	**vaquero**
hogan	**pueblo**		

The old man sat on his horse. Across the road were empty homes made of mud

bricks called _____. No one lived in the _____ anymore.

The Anasazi who once lived there had left the village long ago. The old man was

a _____ sent by his church to bring its beliefs to the Navajo. He had

just returned from visiting a Navajo family in their one-room _____.

Now, as he rested, the _____ climate made him thirsty. As he took

a drink of water, the old man looked up and saw a _____ riding toward

him. The cowboy stopped to say hello. The old man returned the greeting, then rode

on toward his mission.

Notes for Home: Today your child learned to choose vocabulary words by using clues in a story about life in the old Southwest.
Home Activity: Browse the Internet or newspapers and magazines with your child to find images of the Southwest. Have your child identify any examples of vocabulary words that you find in the images.

Life in the Southwest
Expository Writing

The lives of Native Americans in the old Southwest were very different from the
lives of the Spanish who explored and settled there. Think about some of the
similarities and differences these two groups shared. Write an essay to describe the
similarities and differences between the everyday lives of Native Americans and the
Spanish in the early Southwest. Use at least three of the vocabulary words. You
may use an additional sheet of paper.

adobe	pueblo	arid	savanna	hogan
viceroy	missionary	vaquero	aqueduct	

_____

_____

_____

_____

_____

_____

_____

_____

_____

_____

_____

_____

_____

 Notes for Home: Today your child wrote an essay comparing and contrasting the lives of
Native Americans and Spanish settlers in the early Southwest.
Home Activity: Describe to your child what life was like when you were his or her age.
Encourage your child to compare and contrast today's lifestyle to your past.

adobe

pueblo

arid

savanna

gusher

refinery

hogan

a Spanish word that means "village," and which refers to some Native American groups in the Southwest

a kind of mud brick

a grassy plain with few trees

dry, but not desert-like

a factory that separates crude oil into different groups of chemicals

an oil well that produces a large amount of oil

a one-room Navajo home with a door facing east

viceroy

missionary

vaquero

tallow

homestead

aqueduct

a person sent by a religious organization to spread its beliefs

an early governor of Mexico

animal fat used for making candles and soap

Spanish word for "cowboy"

a pipe used to bring water from a distance

land given to settlers by the United States government if they lived and raised crops on it

Looking at Words

Compound Words

When you recognize part of a compound word, you can often make a prediction of the meaning of the word. Below are the individual words that form compound words from this unit. Match each word with its definition. You may use a dictionary.

timberline	greenhouse	livestock
boom town	ghost town	

1. _____ timber

2. _____ line

3. _____ boom

4. _____ town

5. _____ green

6. _____ house

7. _____ ghost

8. _____ live

9. _____ stock

A. a rapid growth

B. a spirit

C. the color of most growing plants

D. a building in which people live

E. an edge or boundary

F. to be alive

G. the amount one has for use or sale

H. trees or forests with wood for building

I. a place smaller than a city

Based on your understanding of the above words, predict definitions for three of the vocabulary words from the word box.

Word	Predicted Definition
10. _____	_____
11. _____	_____
12. _____	_____

Notes for Home: Today your child identified the meanings of compound words from this unit. **Home Activity:** Look for compound words in books, magazines, and newspapers and work with your child to figure out their meanings.

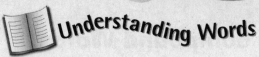

Crossword

Use the vocabulary words from the word box to complete the crossword on page 71.

rain shadow	greenhouse	livestock	totem pole
reforest	timberline	prospector	frigid
boom town	ghost town	potlatch	geyser
magma	lava	tundra	volcano
computer software		international trade	

Across

1. Glass building for growing plants
4. Freezing cold
6. Selling and buying of goods among nations
9. Carved piece of wood with family symbols
10. Programs for an electronic information machine
13. Spring that shoots up hot water and steam into the air
15. Melted rock from a volcano
16. No one lives here anymore
18. Farm animals

Down

2. Plant new trees in the woods
3. The side that gets less water
5. Person who searches for gold
7. Trees do not grow here in the cold
8. Trees do not grow above here
11. Melted rock inside the earth
12. A celebration feast
14. Place that grows fast
17. Hot rock comes from here

© Scott Foresman 4

Notes for Home: Today your child completed a crossword to learn the meaning of vocabulary words.
Home Activity: Work with your child to use each of the vocabulary words in written original sentences.

Vocabulary Workbook

Unit 6   **71**

Traveling West

Narrative Writing

The West is a region of great mountains, beautiful seacoast, and varied climate and landforms. Suppose that you and your family spent last summer vacation exploring the eleven states of the American West. Write a journal entry to describe what you saw during your tour. Use at least five of the vocabulary words. You may use an additional sheet of paper.

timberline	geyser	magma	volcano	lava
tundra	rain shadow	totem pole	potlatch	ghost town

_____

_____

_____

_____

_____

_____

_____

_____

_____

_____

_____

_____

_____

_____

_____

 Notes for Home: Today your child wrote a travel journal entry describing the West based on what was learned in the unit.
Home Activity: Invite your child to read his or her descriptive writing to you. Talk about the liveliest details in your child's writing and if they make you want to visit the West.

timberline

geyser

magma

volcano

lava

tundra

a hot spring that erupts and sends hot water from earth into the air

the elevation on a mountain above which trees cannot grow

a type of mountain with an opening through which ash, gas, and lava are forced

molten rock beneath the surface of the earth

a cold, flat area where trees cannot grow

molten rock that rises and flows on the surface of the earth

frigid

rain shadow

greenhouse

livestock

reforest

totem pole

the side of a mountain chain that receives less precipitation than the other side

very cold

animals raised on farms and ranches for human use

an enclosed structure that allows light to enter and keeps in heat and moisture

a tall post carved with images of people and animals to represent family history

to plant new trees to replace ones that have been cut down

potlatch

prospector

boom town

ghost town

computer software

international trade

© Scott Foresman 4

someone who searches for
valuable minerals

a feast held by Native Americans
of the Northwest to celebrate
important events

a town where all of the people
have moved away

fast-growing town, usually
located near where gold or silver
have recently been discovered

trade between different countries

programs that help computers
perform certain functions